Acceptable Contamination

Larry D. Palmer, Sr.

Acceptable Contamination

Published by Kingdom Kaught Publishing, LLC
Denton, Maryland U.S.A.

Printed in the U.S.A.

Copyright © 2017 by Larry D. Palmer, Sr.

All rights reserved. No part of this book may be reproduced or transmitted in any form or by any means without written permission of the author.

Scripture quotations noted KJV are from the King James Version. Scripture quotations noted NIV are from the HOLY BIBLE: NEW INTERNATIONAL VERSION ®. Copyright © 1973, 1978, 1984 by International Bible Society. Used by permission of Zondervan Publishing House. All rights reserved.

Edited by Sarah Gardner

Library of Congress Control Number: 2017931213

ISBN 9780998210025

I dedicate this book to my wife of over 40 years. She is a superb helpmeet and my best friend. Brenda and I were so young when we decided to marry. Her untiring support and unwavering confidence in me has made life easy; especially for me. She has given me more than I can ever give in return. She sacrificed her dreams and aspirations to follow me around the world as I served 30 years in the United States Air Force.

Every achievement I accomplished was due to her encouragement and inspiration. She continues to undergird me now that we are working together in the vineyard of the Lord. Her continuous sage counsel to young men and women is simply phenomenal. Her supporting role as First lady and minister of the Gospel once again makes it pleasing for me to pastor the members of Israel Total Life Ministries. The Lord blessed us to have two children… both boys …now men, and eight grandchildren from those unions.

Thank you, Babe!

Table of Contents

Introduction 7

Chapter One - MY GENESIS 11

Chapter Two - SPIRITUAL WICKEDNESS 29

Chapter Three - MARRIAGE GOD'S WAY 39

Chapter Four - COMPROMISING LIFE 49

Chapter Five - RELATIONSHIPS CHALLENGED 57

Chapter Six - THE FAMILY 65

Chapter Seven - LIVING WATER VERSUS WATER TO LIVE 69

Chapter Eight - DRIFT 75

Chapter Nine - A FAD WITH NO FAVOR 87

Introduction

As early as I can recall as a child we were taught to be aware of our surroundings and food intake because of possible contaminating sources. In my youthful years we seemed not to worry about worms in apples and candy that fell to the floor; we simply brushed off enough dirt to consume the valued sweet treat. We were basically naïve to the potential contaminants that soon would plague our innocent world.

Drugs though they existed were not dominant. Incestuous relationships though they existed were hidden in dark places, but never openly admitted. Abortions were unheard of though they were performed. Homosexuality, certainly a taboo, was in the closet deep in the corner. No one would dare to admit being gay or lesbian. Alcoholism seemed commonplace, but little did we know that it was also a disease, not just drunkenness. Teenage pregnancy out of wedlock was an embarrassment to the family and the community frowned on such unacceptable practices. These unscrupulous acts only serve as the tip of the iceberg and represent a small percentage of contaminants we face today.

These deeds when placed under the microscope reveal the real weapons of mass destruction of every nation, and affect generation after generation. They are a strategic plan of self-destruction. If there is not a weapon formed that can penetrate the armor that surrounds you; what other method can wreak havoc in the lives of those who serve God? I submit one enemy....... You! Journey this path with me and see where it leads. Perhaps ... just perhaps as we travel together our eyes will

Acceptable Contamination

be opened to a more innocent weapon that is subtly destroying the very fabric of our existence.

The Church is not exempt from being contaminated by outside sources. In fact it appears to be the target of it all. True Christians believe that the Bible is the source by which all other things are measured. If that is truly our benchmark, then purity is found and all truths are derived from this source.

There are many translations of the Bible and quite frankly there are more than enough contaminated versions out there that move to make unacceptable things in the sight of God acceptable in society. I must admit the works of these resources are somewhat convincing and from a novice standpoint seem to rationally convince the reader that their version is closest to the heart of God's Word. So before simply accepting the writings of everything written, do your due diligence.

Look closer to investigate where the truth really lives.

> *"Do your best to present yourself to God as one approved, a worker who has no need to be ashamed, rightly handling the word of truth."*[1]
> (2 Timothy 2:15) ESV

We will also examine the following definitions of the words: *acceptable*, and *contamination*.

---

[1] *The Holy Bible: English Standard Version.* 2001 (2 Timothy 2:15). Wheaton: Standard Bible Society.

Introduction

ACCEPTABLE

ac·cept·a·ble

Adjective: **acceptable**

Able to be agreed on; suitable.

"has tried to find a solution **acceptable to** everyone"

Adequate; satisfactory. As in
"an acceptable substitute for champagne"
Synonyms: satisfactory, adequate, reasonable, quite good, fair, decent, good enough, sufficient, sufficiently good, fine, not bad, all right, average, tolerable, passable, middling, moderate; "an acceptable standard of living"

Pleasing; welcome. As in
"Some coffee would be most acceptable"
able to be tolerated or allowed.
"Pollution in the city had reached four times the acceptable level."
Synonyms: bearable, tolerable, allowable, admissible, sustainable, justifiable, defensible. As in
"The risk had seemed acceptable at the time."

CONTAMINATION

It is the presence of a minor and unwanted constituent, contaminant or impurity in a material, physical body, natural environment, workplace, etc.

To make (something) dangerous, dirty, or impure by adding something harmful or undesirable to it.

To soil, stain, corrupt, or infect by contact or association (bacteria contaminated the wound) to make inferior or impure by admixture iron; "contaminated with phosphorus."

To make unfit for use by the introduction of unwholesome or undesirable elements.

Chapter One

MY GENESIS

It seemed to be all too surreal; I was born in the small town of Princeton, West Virginia, where I enjoyed a blissful childhood. I grew up in a small two-bedroom home with a loft that housed six boys while the two girls shared a bedroom downstairs. We were poor but I did not know it; therefore no one could define me as being so. The environment was as though we lived in a huge playground. The land was overflowing with what we thought of as milk and honey. The entire neighborhood ate from the fruit of the land. Grapes, apples, pears, strawberries, blackberries, walnuts, and an eatable unknown to many called chinquapins (a type of chestnut) were plentiful. Gardens and livestock were shared.

Now that I write about it and compare it to the many other parts of the world that I've experienced, I realize that we were poor… really poor. I did not know it at the time because we were also rich in spirit. I felt like I lived in the land of Canaan because my father provided everything we needed.

My father was a genius of a man; a real giant in my eyes and the eyes of others. There was nothing I thought he could not do. After all, he was an airplane pilot, an unimaginable achievement in the fifties for a local African American man, a Negro! He was an auto mechanic, an all-around handy man, carpenter, plumber, electrician, mason, Sunday school superintendent, and public servant that worked on the side of righteousness and justice. He was a teacher and father who mentored eight children and others; and lastly, I remembered him being an accomplished musician.

My father died much too soon at the early age of 52. He experienced a massive cardiac arrest and could not recover. When I was told of his death I simply blanked out all communication denying the fact that my superman was gone. The sting of his death marked the beginning of my realizing that the world had contaminating spirits.

The first contaminating source for me was Anger. I began to dislike everything in seemingly everybody. I could not understand why my father was taken away from me at the peak of my happiness. He seemed bigger than Death. My angry spirit began to take its toll. It started to consume me. My anger grew as I reflected upon other children who had fathers. That dark spirit began to infect my mind. As a result, I suffered setback after setback. As time passed, I sought to replace the hero who had fallen with my oldest brother. He was in the United States Air Force and simply could not fill that void.

It was a tragic time for me and the whole family as we tried to deal with the absence of our dad in each of our own ways. As I look back now I missed hearing my father say things like: "Great job son! That's my boy! I am proud of you." Even the words "You are a man, now." I felt for years that I was cheated of those precious comments that many or perhaps all young men want and need to hear their dads utter.

Chapter One - My Genesis

The anger contaminated my Spirit. Loneliness absorbed my soul, filled my heart with brokenness, and overwhelmed my mind with confusion. Where could I find relief? Who would take the place of the greatest man in the world? When would this tragic moment pass? I tried to replace the pain with sports and other activities to bury each day; it just was not working. As I look back over my life I can vividly see where some of my waywardness evolved.

I remember a great deal of things about the events in my childhood. For example, I recall being a child who would talk back to authority. Not out loud of course; I was smart enough to know that the punishment for being rude would be too severe. I seemed to get away with stuff because I was the youngest of the family. At least that is what I am told by my older siblings. The death of my father intensified my anger and perhaps I got off the hook with some things that I would not have gotten away with if he had been still alive.

My mother was a Super hero, a *Shero*, in her own right. She must have suffered a great deal of pain and agony during that time before she passed away at the age of 83. After all, she had been left to raise eight children without a support system. I remember our lives being subsidized by receiving powered milk, powered eggs and block cheese from an unknown source.

Mother washed and ironed clothes perpetually. She earned income by performing domestic deeds in the local white community. She, too, must have been somewhat of a genius. How is it possible (even by today's standards) to feed nine mouths?! Yet, there was not a time to my recollection that I went to bed hungry.

Acceptable Contamination

My mother was a champion when it came to preparing large meals. She not only cooked for our household, she somehow fed others that stopped by (all too frequently) for a visit. We enjoyed such delicious meals as spaghetti and sauce, or bean pies, pinto beans and cornbread. On special occasions we shared chicken, and seemingly always had a dessert. Looking back now it just seems all too incredible!

When you have a house full of children and limited space to move around, organization is paramount. Every family member had chores to perform and excuses were not acceptable. As the youngest, my job was to work the pedals of the Singer sewing machine. Daily as it seemed, I was called upon to pump the pedals of the sewing machine. Rhythm was essential and I had it down pat. I also had to help fold the unending supply of clothes from the laundry my mother cleaned and mended.

We did not have running water and very few homes possessed in- door bathrooms. Yeah, you guessed it, we used outhouses. No lights at night and the hut set quite a ways from the house, for obvious reasons. You learned quickly to take care of business before the sunset.

Father's passing sent us all into a tailspin. Every morning as we all worked through our grief, I remember eating what we called "Cathead" biscuits and gravy. We referred to the biscuits as a cathead due to the size of the biscuit and the gravy was sopped up filling our empty stomachs. On school days we ate puffed rice or simply rice and milk with toast. Meat was saved mostly for Sundays. Once a year in the fall (specifically in November just before Thanksgiving), there was a neighborhood event: hog killing. If you worked you received a portion of the

Chapter One - My Genesis

spoil. My assignment was scraping the hair from the hogs' skin all day long, and I mean from sun-up to sunset.

It was acceptable at the time for an eight-year-old boy to experience anger related to his missing father. The angry spirit haunted me day after day. As much as I tried to shake it that spirit remained alive and well. It took years for the spirit to be arrested.

Finally, I remember the occasion when there was some sort of peace from the awful experience with my father's death. Today, I am able to review the past and pinpoint the source of my healing. I had an awesome experience with Jesus!

I have learned that the scriptures are the most powerful and fulfilling works on earth. Here is why!

> Jeremiah 29:11 *"For I know the plans I have for you,"* declares the LORD, *"plans to prosper you and not to harm you, plans to give you hope and a future."*

When I thought all hope was gone and my Hero taken away, God was working things out on my behalf.

As time passed, I entered back into the world of being fulfilled by my surroundings and managed to get on with life. Throughout the day as we played, we used to drink water from homes that had hoses and from creeks that ran crystal clear from the mountains. Never in my wildest imagination could I have conceived or believed that people would pay for bottles of water. My friends and I used to laugh at the relatives from the city that collected water from the local springs. It was all too normal to us. Even in the summer months the water was cold and always refreshing. We did not realize what we had! Neither did we realize that others knew what we had and sought to market it.

The dream life was all too good and suddenly, almost overnight contaminating sources began to surface. Business people started to migrate into the small town. New homes started to chip away at our daily resources. The fruit trees and grape vines started to disappear. Suddenly the water was no longer healthy to drink. We could drink only tap water now. The contamination was acceptable after all we were growing as an economy and changes were signs of progress, but at what expense? This for me was the eye opener for *"acceptable contamination."*

In the small town of Princeton, life in the early sixties was not a cakewalk. Segregation was the normal way of life from the movie theaters to the shopping arenas. All too often people would remind you about staying in your place. The acceptability of that era however started to erode. Dr. Martin Luther King Jr., Malcolm X, and other popular African American icons stirred a fire in the bellies of so many young and old Americans who long awaited change in our society.

The acceptable ways were dying out and color barriers slowly began to shift. Though I mentioned a few names, I realize it was the hand of the Almighty God extended to His people for peace, righteousness and justice. The hearts and minds of those who hated one another were now being integrated into schools and dorms. How were we going to make it all work? Who would give in and sacrifice the old way of life? It is yet to me a mystery how we asked God for blessings and when HE answered our petitions we complained about how He gave it to us.

Chapter One - My Genesis

As a young child I went to an all-black school, attended an all-black church, ate at an all-black restaurant, sang in an all-black choir, played with an all-black football team (which was never defeated as much as I can remember), and went to an all-black college. I had only been around black people! My first experience with a white male was my football coach. Though he was Italian, he was still considered white to us. As strange as it may seem and sound, the black world was not beneficial for my growth in the real world. Therefore I could surmise that my young spirit was contaminated with hatred and a belief that anyone other than a black person would hold me down.

As time changed, so did my view of the world around me. I began to see things differently. If a shift were going to be made in my life it would have to come from within and not by the hands or control of others. Were all white people blue-eyed devils? Or was my perspective clouded so badly that this dark and wicked thought would haunt me forever? I discovered while there was truly hatred among society during the dark ages of the 1950's and sixties and some of the seventies that my battle extended far beyond the race factor. Nevertheless I still had to battle the race discrimination act. My first integration experience came when I attended the 9th grade. It was a total shock to me that not one African-American former schoolmate was in any of my classes! I got to get a glimpse of them during the changing of classes, but we didn't intermingle until lunchtime or football practice. Our social times were cut off, the atmosphere was totally different, and the academic side was challenging. After all we had been receiving second hand and past edition books. This shift in culture caused several of my schoolmates to drop out of school. The pressure was just too great for them. That year passed with a great deal of depressing moments. The 10th grade (then called the first year of high school) proved to be a little less tense. The curriculum was easier to grasp. If you wanted to play sports you had to face the same discriminatory challenges as in past years. I chose not to go through the pain of playing behind other athletes that were notably less talented.

In the middle of my 10th grade year the spirit that rested in the school system for years faced opposition through an organized walk out. The blatant acts of prejudice that flooded the hallways and classrooms and accepted as normal had to be uprooted.

The rules (as we understood them) stated that the schools had to be integrated. This meant that everyone of color had to be onboard to make the school board superintendents listen to our demands. To our surprise it worked! We protested the unfair treatment of black (then Negro students) and turned the tables on blatant discrimination.

For example, small things like selecting cheerleaders were done by majority vote. Of course being less than ten percent of the school population yielded little chance of the black voice or vote making a difference in the system. We were able to change the system by selecting cheerleaders by percentage vote. This meant the playing field was somewhat leveled by increasing the ratio of voting power per minority student. This method resulted in allowing one black cheerleader to participate on the cheer leading squad. We had pulled up a root of prejudice from the garden of discrimination! Soon other clubs were integrated

Chapter One - My Genesis

by this method to include the Key Club and other private clubs that once only served white students. The surprising resistance came from the alumni and not the students. As time passed, both black and white students began to correspond with one another without taking offense. The 11th and 12th grades of my high school years were a little more pleasant. Not to say that the prejudice aroma had dissipated because it hadn't. All sports teams were still limited to only a few minority players being highlighted. It was simply inconceivable or imaginable to think that teams would be made up of a majority of Black students even if the talent was clearly there! For example, the basketball team had an unwritten rule that the ratio was not to exceed what was known as three /two.

When first hearing this rule I thought it was a defensive tactic or strategy to defend against the opponent. It did not take long to figure out that it really meant only two black players could be on the floor at any given time in the game, regardless of the stakes. Far too many of the great minority athletes did not reach the college-level teams due to the consistent and inequitable treatment simply because of the color of their skin. Upon graduating I decided to try my hand at college. I spent the summer doing odd jobs in effort to raise money to pay for my tuition. I had my eyes on Marshall University in Huntington, West Virginia, but as the school year quickly approached my dreams of playing football for that university faded. I tried multiple support systems, grants, and other avenues to get into Marshall, all to no avail. In November of that year a small airplane crashed killing all 70 plus passengers aboard...the Marshall football team. They had been returning from an

Acceptable Contamination

Eastern Carolina game. The entire college campus was in an uproar. It was as though all hope was gone and life was at a standstill. Needless to say, I felt sick, confused, and emotionally a mess.

I attended Bluefield State College for a short season. My aspirations to finish college were momentarily destroyed. It appeared to be too many things working against me. The jobs in these small towns were scarce and the pay was minimal. Unfortunately my inability to keep up with financial obligations and the Draft drove me into the Armed Services of my choice. For me, there was no way out but to join the military.

I selected the United States Air Force as my primary choice. It was one of the best decisions that I've ever made. I was a fast learner and performed my job with excellence. My original intention was to stay in the United States Air Force only four years but, I adjusted well and began to enjoy the benefits of being an Airman. With that I decided to stay another four years, and as time passed I got married and had two children. After being mentored and meeting many friends my wife and I decided that this would be a great career. My first assignment was in Bunker Hill, Indiana, later called Grissom Air Force Base. Somehow in my mind I thought the United States Air Force would level the playing field for all who wore the uniform. It only took a little while to find out that was far from the truth. There were not many young Black airmen in my group who became propulsion mechanics.

I found myself once again surrounded by a great majority. My scores were average or just above average as I studied relentlessly just to be at the same level as my peers. Though I

Chapter One - My Genesis

was qualified and exceeded all standards, I was still not afforded the opportunity to work on jet engines. I was assigned to what was called the Tool Crib to hand out tools to those less qualified. Yet, I stayed the course, and I wore my uniform with pride.

It took almost 17 months for me to escape what seemed to be a prison sentence for being African American. As I look back over that timeframe I clearly understand now the Scripture, Genesis 50:20: "As for you, you meant evil against me, but God meant it for good…"

Sometimes things happen in our lives that break our hearts or steal our joy. In those moments it is so easy for us to forget that God has a hand in every part of our lives. He knows what we are going to think before we think it and He knows every beat of our hearts. God has a purpose for everything, even the things in your life that seem to take your breath away and break your heart.

It had become an acceptable practice to put young Black airmen in the tool crib to stagnate their growth. As the Lord would have it, I excelled in producing accessory kits for engine buildup issued only from the tool crib. After performing this job for over 16 months I was released to work on the floor. Wow, I finally was being introduced to what I came into the Air Force to do! My fellow airmen had a sizable jump on me, so I had to spin up quickly and work three times as hard to survive. By this time I had gotten promoted against the odds and I became one of the few Black crew chiefs. From my experience of building up engine kits I knew the accessory engine buildup like the back of my hand. That was some 40 years ago. I can still remember some of the national stock numbers associated with the parts, today.

Acceptable Contamination

The base was in the vicinity of Peru Indiana. A city then governed by people who cared little for the Black race. I distinctly recall an incident in one of the grocery stores close to our trailer park dwelling. I went into the store to grab a gallon of milk and perhaps a few other items. I gathered the desired items and proceeded to the register. Once in line a white person stepped in front of me and the cashier waited on him as if I was not there. I was quite militant at that particular time and far from being saved. I uttered a few choice words to let the folks know my displeasure. As I left the store I noticed a march of the Klu Klux Klan (KKK) on the street. I could think of nothing but the safety of my young family awaiting my return to the vehicle. We returned home thinking when will it all end?

To this day in 2016, though many will disagree, the hatred still exists. I transferred out of Indiana to Columbus, Ohio. Wow, what a change! It is here that I discovered that there was hope for our culture and perhaps, just perhaps one could experience an equitable shot of getting promoted and recognized for service provided.

A decade would pass as I kept striving to serve my country and be a representative of United States Air Force. I was selected Airman of the Quarter regularly and had the proud honor of acquiring the Master Technician badge worn only by a few distinct airman! I was promoted several times and I distinctly remember asking the Lord to bless me to make a difference to those things I saw in the military that seemed unjust. I long forgot about the prayer and then it happened. I was selected for the top one percent of the total enlisted force. It was the ultimate rank that many strived to achieve! It would

Chapter One - My Genesis

take me a year to pin on the rank due to being so young or shall I say junior to those that tested.

The months passed slowly as I anxiously waited for my number to pop up. I was eligible for slots held by Chiefs including the highest enlisted position on base. Just for kicks I applied for it to see all that was involved in being the top guy. You guessed it ... I was selected over thirty-four other candidates! My prayer was answered and now I had to quickly assert myself as being qualified for the job. I took over the position but had not yet sewn on the stripe. Needless to say that drew a massive amount of attention!

Dover was a tough assignment. The aircraft maintenance units (AMU) were named to celebrate the KKK. Whether on purpose or someone had a point to prove, I am not sure. I do know that the names made it difficult for many of the airmen to serve (both black and white). One of the first orders of business was to remove the dark cloud of any prejudgment from all units. It meant that the AMUs had to go through a paradigm shift and any paraphernalia along with it. The units use to pride themselves in handing out wizard and dragon statues to those departing the unit. Unbelievable! I thought, "Why hasn't someone raised the flag on this mess or gone to Equal Employment Opportunity to resolve the issue?"

It did not take long for me to figure out that the majority of those functioning under this duress were afraid or unfortunately accepted this as the norm. Thank God for a Wing Commander who had the mettle to make immediate changes after selecting me as his go-to Chief. The AMU names were immediately changed to Red, White and Blue. Very appropriate wouldn't you say for the patriotism needed for the maintenance units? Needless to mention my job for the next couple of years was to combat the paradigm that had rested there for so many years.

I must say the shift in leadership was not well received and the culture swing caused many to retire or make career moves. There was one great chief that I knew had my back without compromise and at the time he was the top rank man to sew on chief stripes. He sat in for me in my absence from the base and I could always trust that things were in order upon my return.

It has been almost 22 years since that period and only a few years ago my son landed an assignment at Dover. One would think that the old railroad gang was far gone by now but you guessed it; he just by the pulling the short straw worked in an area where there was a remnant of those who served years ago that still held on to the old culture. Some contaminating spirits go dormant for years waiting for the opportunity to strike. It did not take long for the now retired remnant to discover who my son was! He suffered backlash for being the son of one who dismantled and surely disappointed multiple homesteaders whom ruled for a while. Eventually because of attrition, my son was removed from unjust and unfair treatment. The clean-up took a little while to mend broken and wrecked careers along the way.

It was tough to say the least, but the Lord held true to His promise and I did all to hold true to my prayer of helping the less fortunate. I was the first African American Command Chief to hold that position at two different Air Force bases. My career ended there and what a great sense of accomplishment!

Chapter One - My Genesis

A Quick Look Back

As a retired veteran over the years I found that resources and man-hours were simply wasted as a result of not following the basic rules of engagement. There were of course, individuals who without any research or particular skill thought they knew how to do the job better, take short cuts that either placed their fellow man in harm's way, or perhaps never really captured the basic method of performing the task. Before entering the military those people thought rules were something that others had to follow and embrace. They might have encountered home rules, school rules, a few college rules that were enforced, but while growing up they followed rules vaguely, if at all.

There was one rule that demanded my attention after finishing high school and that was the military Draft. No one wanted to be known as a draft dodger and neither did I. Every male between the age of 18 and 26 was expected to serve his country, especially during time of war. One way to delay or perhaps totally get out of serving immediately after graduating from high school was to attend college. One had to take full-time classes and maintain a decent grade point average to be exempt from the draft. I recall the draft notices throughout the campus. Young men upset because they had to go against their will into the military (mainly the army) to fight a war no one seemed to clearly understand. I was doing well for a while and then my financial resources began to plummet. I faced withdrawal due to insufficient funds to support my college dreams. That meant my draft notice was on the way. This is how it all began.

Acceptable Contamination

I had a close friend whom I confided in and he had worked out a way to beat the system. I received my notice and was desperate to get out of serving especially in the Army which was sending soldiers straightway to Vietnam. My good friend coached me in how you get out of the service call. He explained that he had gone to the recruitment station and took the AFOQT test in less than five minutes. Of course he failed and was not qualified to go into any branch of service.

As an upcoming and somewhat smart college student, I asked, "How did you know how to answer the questions incorrectly?" He replied, "I just went into the testing room, received my test like all the rest in the place and went down the answer block marking A B C D throughout the test." He said he failed big time. It sounded pretty good to me, especially based on the time I spent trying to pass my college examines, so I attempted the same theory and took the test in less than three minutes.

Anxiously awaiting my bad news the recruiter calls and informed me that I passed the test. I rebelled and angrily exclaimed 'no way!' I even threw my friend under the bus without naming him and said "He took the test and failed; how could I have possibly passed?" You can imagine the recruiter probably smiled as he answered, "We do not give the same test to everyone. Welcome and congratulations. You are going to love your experience and we are, too!" I think that was the very last time I disrespected the military uniform.

After a few months of delayed enlistment, I succumbed to joining the USAF. It seemed I tried everything to avoid what God had planned for me. As a young militant and now college

Chapter One - My Genesis

dropout, the military option was the ultimate choice. After all what could they teach me? I viewed myself as being in great shape and relatively intelligent. 'This is really going to be a breeze...' I thought.

On May 7th I headed to Basic Military Training on Lackland Air Force Base, in San Antonio, Texas. Everything was foreign to me. We all strategically arrived in the middle of the night to face the first wave of rules. They were clearly articulated and very loudly explained. At this juncture one would nearly do anything. Just let us get some sleep. I recall going to bed around 3:30 that morning only to be awakened around 5:30 to meet the second wave of rules. The yelling and cursing and demands were overwhelming, but I survived and even thrived after embedding in my mind that failure was not an option. Disorganized and disoriented we all fell into a pitiful formation. The new instructor shouted louder than those in the unbearable hours before. We were allowed to eat and immediately following, and yep, you guessed it, get set for our next rule play. Everyone had to look alike... no respect for persons. Everyone received the same haircut (bald), the same color underwear (white), the same uniforms: blues and green fatigues.

We were going through our sterilization process. You were considered a nobody unless you were told otherwise. Upon looking back, it was a clever strategy that still remains in use today. And so our training began, day and night; unforgettable stories that will last a lifetime. Eight and one half weeks passed and what a transformation! We were all off to our technical schools to gather more military bearing and train for our individual specialties.

Acceptable Contamination

There were only a few acceptable rules now; the ones you were told were acceptable. If you were going to survive in military life ...follow the rules. Do not bend them or for sure do not break them.

Chapter Two

SPIRITUAL WICKEDNESS

"Do You See What God Sees"

We serve during a time where everyone wants to be noted as the head of the movement, congregation, organization, or simply the CEO of something. Far too often you may hear the song ring out that 'I just cannot work for someone else. I have to be my own boss.' Usually when I hear those words the thought that follows is that 'no one should be following you either.' A leader who does not know how to follow is a train wreck in motion. Soon the leader and whoever follows his/her flawed leadership will sadly derail.

People who invest and unfortunately crumble under poor leadership are damaged for years and often times for life. The scars of failed leadership are in many cases irreversible. Once a person is deeply led astray it takes a miracle to get them to trust again and rely on or have confidence in leadership. Church leadership is not exempt from experiencing this same phenomenon.

In many cases, the Church has the same issues as those of the world. It really should not be but we have to face reality and call a spade a spade. Today there is nearly a church on every corner. This reality should be favorable for the Kingdom of

God. Instead we notice divided communities, half with doctrines and in some cases the practice of witchcraft and other forces under the cover of church. Contaminated spirits are running rampant in the house of God and mainly in the leadership positions. Why? Perhaps it is because the head is sick and there is no soundness in it.

> Isaiah 1:5-6 — *"Why should ye be stricken any more? ye will revolt more and more: the whole head is sick, and the whole heart faint. From the sole of the foot even unto the head there is no soundness in it; but wounds, and bruises, and purifying sores."*

The wisdom from our forefathers was passed down throughout the years. Although in many cases, the words may not have been totally correct, their spirits were right and God blessed them to relay to us sound doctrine. Some others who are called or say they are called to the ministry might quickly depart from the faith.

There are many reasons that people fall away from the authority of the Church. Listed are just a few:

1. I have outgrown the ministry
2. The Lord is calling me to Pastor
3. My season here is up
4. Where I come from we did it like this
5. I cannot spread my wings here
6. If I were in charge I would do it like this
7. I did not understand the weight of the ministry

Chapter Two - Spiritual Wickedness

Today unfortunately, we face a new generation of preachers that know best before they learn what the best is. The acceptance of worldly spirits rule in many of instances and when these spirits grow strong in the body they take root and possess the entire body.

Here are just a few of the spirits being accepted and eventually taking permanent habituation in the Church:

1. Word Contamination in the pulpit
2. Life Contamination in the congregation
3. Praise Dancers with no Spirit
4. Homosexuals (better known as the alternative lifestyle) in leadership positions
5. Music Department for hire
6. Cell groups …cannot work with others just my few
7. Greeters but no commitment
8. Ushers, but cannot usher in HIS presence
9. Speaking in tongues but cannot speak to one another
10. Armor bearers have turned into Armed bearers

All facets of ministry are seeking the praises of men and not God. Where does it all end? Are we to accept the worldly measures and give up on sanctifying the Church? Should we not serve the Lord and keep His commandments or fold up holiness and join such a minority and give in to sin?

King David's spirit was contaminated by Bethsheba's beauty and his lust for her nakedness would lead to the death of her husband. Uriah was clueless as to why this ill fate had fallen on

Acceptable Contamination

him. It serves us to know that our paths are sometimes carved by the wickedness of others. Bethsheba's household was destroyed and she lost the child conceived by King David. Moreover, King David lost his closeness to God and felt the pain of losing his anointing.

It simply cannot be so that God is pleased with our lack of love and sensitivity to Him. Therefore we should further examine these acts of wickedness. Notice that there is always an ingredient in any recipe that if it doesn't belong it will spoil the intended outcome. David consciously decided to compromise his kingship and lower his standards even to the point of taking another man's life. Psalm 51 describes his feeling best.

> *"Create in me a clean heart and renew the right spirit within me, Do not cast me from your presence, or take your Holy Spirit from me, Restore to me the Joy of my salvation and grant me a willing spirit, to sustain me." (Psalm 51)*

King David's act of unfaithfulness to God haunted him for the remainder of his days. It is certainly a hard lesson, but one worth learning.

Judas' (one of Jesus' disciples) spirit was contaminated by money. Many think that he was not really for Jesus in the first place. While that point may have some merit, it overlooks the point of Judas being chosen like the others and perhaps, just perhaps it was indeed the plan of God. After all he personally witnessed Jesus at work in communities healing, delivering and casting out demons.

Chapter Two - Spiritual Wickedness

Judas was infected with a virus of disbelief and acted accordingly by selling Jesus out. His spirit was so disturbed after realizing whom he had betrayed that he decided to take his own life. Instead of asking Jesus to forgive him and heal his unbelief, he decided to take things into his own hands and settle the matter himself through hanging.

This Suicidal spirit is alive and well, today. People who turn their back on Jesus and somewhere along the way realize it still try to take matters into their own hands. When the pressures of life are far too great for some to handle the easy way out seems to be death by suicide. For the true believer there is another way. We know that there is nothing too hard for God. Scripture declares it in this manner:

"When my heart is overwhelmed lead me to the rock that is higher than I." Psalm 61:2

"If you can have it He can heal it."

Potiphar's Wife

Potiphar's wife's spirit was contaminated by lying and lust before she met Joseph. Joseph's story begins in Genesis chapter 37.

Joseph had escaped the attempt of his own brothers to take his life. They had become so enraged with his vision of one day ruling over them and the favor their father showed to Joseph that they threw him into a pit with the intention to leave him there for dead. A secondary plan surfaced and Joseph's brothers sold him into slavery instead. Joseph's brothers collaboratively agreed to lie to their father as to the whereabouts of Joseph.

Remember becoming an accessory to anything unjust causes your spirit to become unclean. Though he was rescued by one of his eldest brothers; he was still sold into slavery and never expected to be seen again. Human trafficking seemed to be a common practice in that day. Something that still exists and it yet has a devastating effect on the unfortunate people involved.

Joseph was tossed around with inhuman concern. Potiphar, however, saw something that others failed to see in Joseph. Unfortunately, so did Potiphar's wife. The spirit of Lust overcame her and she uncontrollably sought Joseph's attention. Day after day Potiphar's wife pursued Joseph to sleep with her, but Joseph refused. Perhaps this spirit just manifested itself, but somehow as one reads the story it appears to be an old lustful demon. The boldness of Potiphar's wife seemed too common. Perhaps she had released this spirit in the past.

Joseph now accustomed to fighting demons and being faithful to his master was able to resist the multiple attempts of Potiphar's wife to sleep with him. Her spirit was surely twisted, one that would make a popular series for soap operas today. Being that she could not have her way with him, she acquired another spirit …Lying. She accused Joseph of trying to have his way with her and Potiphar reluctantly had him thrown in jail. Joseph once again found himself in a pit similar to the one his brothers dropped him into because they despised his favor with their father.

Chapter Two - Spiritual Wickedness

Lot's Wife

Little is known about Lot's wife. She is only known for the looking back when instructed not to do so. Perhaps she was so attached to the dwelling place that she could not help but take one last glance at what used to be called home. It is unknown what her input was when Lot offered his daughters to the men attacking their home. She is just the lady who turned into a pillar of salt. We do know that she lacked obedience. Some call it curiosity, but whatever it was the spirit that contaminated her ability to be obedient caused her to die.

Things we once enjoyed have a way of haunting us to the point where we habitually remind ourselves of the good old days. For example, we often drift back and reminisce on the things we use to do when we were young. Family reunions are perfect forums for recalling off-taste things that are funny to us now. Stealing and cheating were commonplace. But there were more intense mistakes we made in the days of old for which we are yet paying the price. Bearing children out of wedlock and experimenting with dangerous drugs which changed our behaviors and caused scars for life. These are just a couple of things that if we could turn back the hands of time we may decide to take another route.

Regardless how much fun and how innocent we may believe our unsaved lives were; we now know that those days were damaging to our relationship with the Lord. It is only by the grace of God that many of us survived and escaped the grips of death.

Acceptable Contamination

The thought of looking back and going back should raise a flag to leave the past in the past and press toward the future. The scripture states it this way:

> *"Brethren, I count not myself to have apprehended it, but this one thing I do: forgetting those things which are behind, and reaching forth unto those things which are before, I press toward the mark of the prize of the high calling of God in Christ Jesus."*
> (Philippians 3:13-14)

The throwback times and the "use to be able to" syndrome captivate us all at times, but to allow the era to contaminate the spirit once again is cause for repentance in the sight of God. Perhaps the answer is to remember but not to rewind. Don't look back!

Judas the Disciple

Judas is the classic case of a turncoat. He followed Jesus like the other disciples, yet a spirit took over his intellectual process and caused him to turn on the very One Who loved and cared for him the most. I once preached a message titled "What happened to Judas?" While studying the scriptures I gave it my best shot to put myself in Judas' shoes. He like the other disciples saw the works and miracles that Jesus performed. He experienced firsthand the Spirit of Christ for himself. The spirit that captured his thoughts sent him into a state of envy and spite toward Jesus.

Chapter Two - Spiritual Wickedness

This spirit is certainly not an unfamiliar one. We engage with people daily that carry this same contaminated mindset. They start out with you giving every indication that they fit into your vision, only to find out later in heat of the battle that they cannot go into the fight with you.

I must admit there was a point in the story that I felt sorry for Judas as I do for others who make a choice to side with the enemy. Judas had realized after accepting 30 pieces of silver that he had indeed sold the Savior out. He even tried to return the money and redeem himself, but it was too late. If we examine ourselves closely, we often travel the same path as the unpopular Judas. All too often we carry the name of Christian, but do not have the nature of Christ. We find ourselves compromising the Word of God and allowing too many invitations to the world to crucify our Lord and cheaply sell out our beliefs.

What happened to Judas? He was infected with an evil spirit and took the low road of serving Christ. Though many despise the name, there are still many that unknowingly take on the same character. Examine yourself and make sure you are not doing the same.

Haman/Mordecai

The story of Haman in the book of Esther is certainly a classic. Like many other commanders his plan was to be promoted, be noted for his authority, and earn the respect of those in the city. Unfortunately, he chose the wrong path as do many who seek to make it to the top of the chain. Haman's source of contamination came through the spirits of Hatred,

Arrogance and Ignorance. He had everything a Commanding officer could hope to gain with the exception of the loyalty of one man…Mordecai. His hatred caused him to make an unwise decision against a people who had done him no harm. His arrogance and pride drove him to attempt to prove a point of having authority and forced respect from all. His ignorance suffocated his ability to think clearly as he sought to destroy a man that was more loyal to the King than he. Unfortunately it all lead to his discredit and ultimately to death. It is a short synopsis of a great biblical story and makes for incredible reading. Throughout each episode one can see the shift of spirits as each character seeks to fulfill its own destiny.

Chapter Three

MARRIAGE GOD'S WAY

"The thief cometh not, but for to steal, and to kill, and to destroy: I am come that they might have life, and that they might have it more abundantly." (John 10:10)

Webster defines marriage as "the state of being united to a person of the opposite sex as husband and wife in a consensual and contractual relationship recognized by law."

Marriage has now been redefined as a uniting of two regardless of sex preference.

The Word of God in Genesis 2:23-24 clearly makes this point:

Acceptable Contamination

> "This at last is bone of my bones and flesh of my flesh; she shall be called Woman, because she was taken out of Man. Therefore a man shall leave his father and his mother and hold fast to his wife, and they shall become one flesh."

The definition of things written in the various dictionaries can and often are rewritten and augmented to meet the needs of society. As a matter of fact the definition of marriage has followed this pattern to describe marriage as "a similar relationship (as husband and wife) between people of the same sex." (Webster)

The confusion of societies all over the world is mounting and many simply believe the end of times is upon us. The scripture declares in the end of time *"There will be evil in the last days and difficult times to come. Men will be lovers of themselves..."* 2 Tim 3:1-2 and

> "And likewise the males, leaving the natural use of the females, burned in their lust one toward another: men with men working that which is unseemly, and receiving in themselves that recompense of their error which was meet." (Romans 1:27)

The times are upon us that the days of old have become the days of now. It seems that we are more apt to accept things that are not just or right before God. The easy way out is to twist the minds of men and women to believe that God is pleased with anything we place before Him. If we cannot change the status of a run-away train we simply increase the speed limit to make it appear normal. In many states blood tests are no longer

Chapter Three - Marriage God's Way

required to determine relationship of those uniting. The age limit to marry is tainted by the lack of rules. It is more acceptable to live together and become common partners than to enter into the covenant of marriage.

As recently as June 26, 2015 the highest court in the nation enacted a law that same sex marriage is allowed in all fifty states of this great nation we call the United States of America. Perhaps this is an indication of the fall of a great nation to blatantly dismiss the commandment of God and decide to take matters into its own hands. It seems to relate to the fall of Rome as great as that city once appeared to be.

Though the law is now the law of the land, it is important (by those who know God) to note that man cannot change the law or principle of God no more than he can change the law of gravity. Regardless of what he calls it or tries to redefine it God's Word will still stand and apply. I heard during a sermon at the most recent church conference I attended that within two decades of the Supreme Court announcement that 100,000 homosexuals will surrender their lives back to Christ. I am not quite sure how that number will be measured or who will keep the count of the souls returned to the Lord but if God allows it will be a monumental shout in the churches of the Living God we serve.

Before the Supreme Court decision was announced I knew in my spirit the outcome. There were just too many signals to affirm what was about to happen. Television shows with homosexual hosts were and still are prevalent. The new modern family which highlights homosexual relationships undoubtedly served as the catapult to prepare the generation for accepting

Acceptable Contamination

homosexual trends. The media amplifies the wave of the next acceptable challenge of God's Voice and His people. Just recently a woman married her dog opening up the door for bestiality! It may be the next wave society has to face if it is not already anchored in the minds of those who want to amplify it.

Celebrities coming out of what they call closet relationships declaring themselves as gays seemingly help set the tone for acceptance. The Supreme Court decision was unveiled and prompted a setback to the nation.

History does seem to repeat itself. In the scriptures the city of Sodom was prone to collapse. The lifestyle we now call alternative was flaming hot and the people had grown accustomed to all that was transpiring. The men of the city had lost their way and when they approached Lot they asked to violate the guest in his home. These were men desiring to violate other men. This action clearly denotes that not only are the minds of these men poisoned by sin, but they wanted to infect anyone who decided to go the other way. Lot tried to calm the crowd by offering his virgin daughters and the men had absolutely no desire for a relationship with females.

Our nation is quickly turning to that style of living once again. Women are leaving the natural use of their bodies at a rapid pace and the men are coming out of the closet (so to speak) as fast as the door can swing. Our children are confused to the exposure of sinful acceptability as they try to balance life, but this acceptable disease is growing too fast. Parents are offering the child the choice of whether to be a boy or a girl regardless of their God-given makeup. The coalition of foolishness is rapidly growing and it is undermining a weak and shameful generation. The answer is and has always been Jesus, but the question still rings… "Who is He?"

Those who are referred to as the millennial society or 'Generation Y,' struggles to trust God, and those serving God. The answer appears to be an actual demonstration of the power of God. I had the opportunity in a meeting with a panel of those from ages 18 to 35 to witness the thoughts of what was expected from the modern Church. To my surprise it was not much different from what we expected when we were in that age group. I noticed that most of the testimonials referred to there being a gap in the young and old worship experience. When asked what can be done to close the gap the overwhelming response was 'to lead and guide us.' It was the exact thing they seemed not to want only minutes before!

After the session was over, I discerned in my spirit that there are a great number of young folks that really love the Lord and want to do the right thing. Unfortunately in many cases some were misguided by what they had seen and been exposed to in the past.

Another strong link to winning millennialism to Christ is the media. We live in a season of information technology and whoever is able to use Google or Twitter or Instagram, Periscope or other methods that sound convincing, captures the attention of thousands and their following grows. Churches are attempting to adjust to the wave of transitions that make the worship experience soothing to the rising generation, but with what sacrifice?

One of the major issues with any generation is having a standard in which to measure righteousness and justice. When either are out of synchronization the balance of life is thrown into chaos. Today we are faced with a host of challenges that cause many of our youth to choose the wrong paths. That is certainly not an excuse for misbehavior, but it does bear weight on the inability for some to be successful in life. For instance, it is almost cool to have a criminal record or to have spent some time in jail. Marriages are occurring for convenience. Children are being born with a slim hope of enjoying both parents through their school-age years. Divorces are commonplace now, and instead of being the exception they have become the rule.

> *"They said to Him, "Why then did Moses command to give her a certificate of divorce and send her away?" He said to them, "Because of your hardness of heart Moses permitted you to divorce your wives; but from the beginning it has not been this way..."*
> (Matthew 19:7-8)

The hearts of men and women are still hard and divorces are on the rise. In times past separation and calling it quits was frowned upon. Now it has become a normal practice both in and outside the walls of the Church. It is all too easy to walk away from the sworn vows made to one another and to God.

Several years ago I found myself talking to a group of guys that I had been playing basketball with and the conversation about marriage surfaced. One of the individuals asked me "How long have you been married?" I responded "38 years." His expression spoke volumes. It was almost as if he was saying without speaking a word; 'are you crazy? You have been married

Chapter Three - Marriage God's Way

to the same women for 38 years!' My emphatic answer was 'yes' and happy to say I am still in love with her.

After conversing more, I learned that many people do not plan to be married for the long run. In other words, to them forever does not last always. It was really as if we were talking about trying out cars and if that model did not work for me trade it in on something different or even worst a newer model. This mindset ruins lives and cripples the family structure. Short-term marital relationships take their toll on the husband and wife, but especially the children, if any. The majority of the children caught in this quandary are rebellious and lose respect for authority. Children subjected to this kind of pressure are known to be mad at the world and defiant to one of the parents they feel responsible for the divorce. You can almost feel the outcry for help and remedy to ease the pain of agony.

Years ago my wife and I had the opportunity to counsel multiple couples over a period of three decades or so. The big three is still the leading cause of marital visits. They are communication, money or sex; not necessarily in that order. Also noteworthy is that 80% of the visitation is made up of Church folks. It is so alarming at times to get the testimony of those who express their love of the Lord, yet complain about the power of that same love.

Deeper counsel consistently reveals a direct correlation with their relationship with Jesus and their relationship with one another. If the Jesus relationship is broken or weak, so follows the broken or weak relationship with one another. It sounds all too simple, but it is all too true.

Acceptable Contamination

Unpacking brokenness is a chore for any counselor. The contaminants of those who visit are so impacted that it often takes hours of constant testimonies and a keen ear to unwind or untangle the good habits or issues from the destructive ones. Some couples have lived with destructive cancers for years and finally are overcome with the collection of unhealthy spirits. The small unacceptable things not dealt with were okay while left alone. When joined forces with new unacceptable issues the weight shifts and the person affected begins to break down. When a case is this hopeless (at least to the minds of those who sat in the chairs) it takes the surgical hand of the Holy Spirit to operate on the sensitive parts of a relationship and to heal body, mind, soul and spirit before the relationship can be restored.

It is alarming to work with couples that have been married 20, 30 and in some cases 40 plus years and still wrestle with the heated subjects of what happened decades ago. It takes the power of the Holy Spirit to hold back the words ... "Are you kidding?!" Things that occurred twenty years ago are yet haunting the relationship.

Can you imagine carrying a demon on your back for such a long period of time and tip toeing around trying not to awaken the spirit? It is like observing a grown man with a pacifier in his mouth or around his neck. It is even contaminating to think that some relationships survive over the years with that kind of stronghold attached to them. They simply work around the issue and not through it.

When the counselees enter the room the counselor knows that they are desperate to get help. For me counseling begins upon entering the room, the body language speaks volumes of

Chapter Three - Marriage God's Way

both. Seating is often another indicator of where the issue may lie. The eyes are of course the windows of the soul so close attention is paid to where they travel. Is the couple reverent to one another or have they thrown in the towel? The hands are nearly a dead giveaway. The wedding rings, which once represented their inseparable promise, are either worn or removed to symbolize the broken bond.

In order to attempt to open the lines of communication, the atmosphere is set through prayer. Usually during that time you can feel the tension. The couple will hold hands or purposely avoid the contact.

Depending on the couple's application submission, reading the wedding vows are a good place to break the ice and get right to the issue at hand. It seldom fails to unravel one of the emotions. Of course, after the ground rules are set it may be wise to let the disgruntled one start off the conversation.

Prepare yourself to offer a keen ear and take notes (copious notes) to avoid missing anything that may be the key element to aiding you in helping the couple to resolve their issue(s). Something has disrupted the relationship and it is your job to identify it and call it out. When seeking to analyze the problem, make absolutely sure you hear and closely weigh both sides of the party lines. Then and only then can you recommend solutions.

Remember that a contaminated spirit can hide for several sessions. Do not be quick to conclude based on things revealed during the first or second session.

Marriage is based on the Word of God and it will take the Word of God to sustain it and insert joy into it. The answer to a loving marital relationship is Christ. It has, will, and always will be the source of an unbreakable bond.

Chapter Four

COMPROMISING LIFE

(Representative)

As a representative of Christ our job in taking on His Name is to re-pre-sent Him. In other words as He is so are we to be. We are the ambassadors of Him who stated in His Word, "For in Him we live and move, and have our being." (Acts 17:28)

One summer afternoon my wife, Brenda, and I decide to travel to Wilmington, Delaware to visit her aunt who had been in an assistance living home for some time. We were still active duty in the military and had traveled extensively throughout our career.

Upon our arrival we found Brenda's eldest aunt surprisingly alert; we renewed relationships that had been fractured for many years. It was truly a family reunion of cousins, aunts, and friends that we had not seen in twenty to thirty years. Some of the folks we had never met or even knew we were related to. All the excitement took our focus off of our Aunt who was declining rapidly. One or two at a time would proceed back to her room to visit of which she knew none when they returned. Dementia had taken its toll to the point where she did not even know her own son.

Brenda and I decided to take our turn in the room where she comfortably lay. As we were approaching an unusual moment unraveled. My wife's aunt with a radiant smile looked up and said, "Here comes the preacher and his wife." She called Brenda and I by name which stunned us both. "How are you all doing?" she said with enthusiasm and a clear mind. Of course we answered "Very well and how are you feeling?" She did not complain at all and beckoned me to come closer to her. I did, and as I bent over to greet her she whispered into my ear two words that resonate even now. "DON'T COMPROMISE!"

Immediately thereafter she returned to her loss of memory stage and I of course was blown away. I could not shake the shortest and most powerful sermon that I had ever heard. Those two words rang out, as they still do, to me over and over again. I talked about it with my wife for weeks. It seemed, and I believe in my spirit, that an angel spoke through her to share a message that will last until eternity for me!

Perhaps you may have encountered the same type of message from an unexpected source that reminds you to reflect upon the Godly image without wavering.

There are times we all fall short of projecting the Christ-like image.

The saying "to save the lost at any cost" is catchy and opens the door to various spirits to enter the Church and in some cases take over the Body of believers. While the cliché sounds wonderful and exciting, much of the principles of God are being sacrificed to simply gather a crowd in the pews. The lost are so confused concerning the standards of the Church that they simply believe it is just another place to get their "groove on." They are known supposedly as spiritual or Holy night clubs. These fashionable establishments are to take the place of the

Chapter Four - Compromising Life

party hangouts. The idea attracts group after group and it does not take long for the same environment to develop. The cunning scheme of the adversary seduces his prey into believing that God wants to be more open to the world and put aside the old way of Holiness. The Body is pulled into believing that this is the new evangelistic method of winning the youth to serve the Lord. Nothing could be further from the truth.

One can notice, if the scales are removed from his eyes, (as it was with Saul on the Damascus road) that the allurement of the enemy is a modified mode of operation, yet the purpose (to rob, kill and destroy) is the same. The tactic remains to draw souls away from God instead of moving souls closer to Him. I realize that there are shifts necessary to attract people to the Lord. Technology is the driving force of how the Word is distributed and that social media is the wave of the future. Got it! I also realize that the Body of Christ must stay in tune with the times and offer more than the spiritual training received from our forefathers. Keeping all that in mind we must still maintain holiness and righteousness before the Lord.

The Church does not have to succumb to allowing out of the closet homosexuals to govern praise teams and strut their unholiness before God. Somehow church leaders are willing to sacrifice obedience to God's Word, putting on blinders and turning faces from what is obvious. The contamination process begins and soon there are multiple spirits in the entire music ministry, not just the praise team. The Word tells us in 1 Corinthians 5:6-8:

Acceptable Contamination

> *"Do you not know that a little leaven leavens the whole lump? Therefore purge out the old leaven, that you may be a new lump, since you truly are unleavened. For indeed Christ, our Passover, was sacrificed for us. Therefore let us keep the feast, not with old leaven, nor with the leaven of malice and wickedness, but with the unleavened bread of sincerity and truth."*

The Dance Ministry

Many people fail to admit that this ministry has to be monitored for Holiness closely, especially if the leader is young and vibrant. I know it is exactly what all ministries desire to have. It is as though the combination could not be better. But wait! The ministry has too many females and very few males. Can males dance before the Lord with passion without being labeled as soft or suspect? Are the females performing to be seen and praised for their talent and moves? Who is minding the store or is it acceptable to just take what is offered in the service? By the way, once the dance is launched it is too late to try to recover.

The subtleness of seduction creeps into the dance ministry. Suddenly the dances are more provocative, the outfits are more revealing and the purpose shifts from praising God to seducing onlookers.

The buffoonery of babies mocking preachers and being allowed to enter into the pulpit to get a few laughs and shout-outs is as infectious as a virus is to a computer. For too many it is seen as cute and entertaining. Again the call is for Holiness, not hilariousness. Just as a CPU crashes when overcome with an uncontrollable virus, thus is the Kingdom when unacceptable spirits remain unchecked.

An Intrusive and Unhealthy Habit

One of the most controversial arguments in and outside of the federal government was the subject of taking cigarette breaks. The smoking habit is known to cause a rift between nonsmokers and those who smoke regularly. In times past it was acceptable to smoke in the office and take as many breaks as you desired. It is almost unheard of now to smoke inside of any building so those who maintain the habit of smoking must revert to smoking in a designated area outside of the work area. The average smoke break is between 10 and 15 minutes, and some smokers delight in smoking two or more cigarettes. If an employee takes two smoke breaks an hour, he or she is only productive a maximum of four hours a day. This becomes the controversy for those who do not smoke. This difficult-to-break habit is known to contaminate the body and the workforce as well.

The short cure to the smoking habit is to "kick the habit." It is much easier said than done I am told being a non-smoker. Perhaps equal break time for those who do not smoke as for those who do would be fair? If that is the answer, then all employees would be non-productive for hours each workday. One would have to double the workforce to get an honest day's work.

Contaminating spirits though they appear innocent create problems even though they may not affect you directly.

Breaking News

The Episcopalian Church has decided to accept same-sex relationships in the church and change the definition of marriage of one man and one woman.

African American churches being burned to the ground as in the days of old has become common practice.

Nine killed in a Bible study gathering by a gunman who sat among the people before slaughtering them.

Though technology has its place, "A robot commits murder and crushes a man at an auto plant." Removing the human factor doesn't come without a price.

The Confederate (Rebel) flag is permanently lowered with honors after 54 years of flying over the state capitol of South Carolina. The flag stood for racism, hatred and pain toward fellowman.

Law enforcement personnel, sworn to protect and defend the public, turn to the dark side and kill innocent men and women.

Teen student refusing to submit to authority is dragged from her classroom chair and thrown to the floor by the school police officer while the teacher and other students calmly watch.

NASCAR racing denounces the rebel flag symbol and some businesses and companies follow suit and appear to wake up from a long sleep.

A United States military base changes the names of the aircraft maintenance units which paralleled the names of the KKK. The Wizards, Dragons and proposed White Nights

Chapter Four - Compromising Life

names were scratched from the books and permanently buried from a unit sworn to protect and serve the nation.

Marijuana is legalized in the state of Colorado and other states. It is a substance known to alter behavior and now it is deemed as a medication.

College football team refuses to play until something is done concerning the racial slurs and unjust treatment of African-American students.

These are just a few of the acceptable contaminants that haunt a nation and cause too many people to view it as normal. We justify it by saying, "If you cannot control it legalize it. If there is no way to stop it, normalize it. If the people rebel keep emphasizing it, eventually the contamination will become a part of life and accepted into the culture."

Chapter Five

RELATIONSHIPS CHALLENGED

Anger is a spirit that will infiltrate the very soul of man and cause him to commit unthinkable sins.

Cain and Abel

The incredible story of these two brothers fit into many of the households today. The majority of what is written does not focus on the great times they must have enjoyed as young boys. The lens seemed to come alive when we focus in on the bad times which caused them to divide. Neither of the sons of Adam and Eve was contaminated by outside influences. So we know they must have existed in the beginning. Cain the eldest son, Genesis 4:8, was infected by the spirit of Jealousy, an ingredient not intended to be used in the recipe of a child of God. He further allowed his jealousy to manifest anger and in his inner rage killed his own brother. What is it that causes us to move so far away from God's intended recipe for our lives?

Abel, on the other hand, is depicted as one who revered the Lord and gave of his first fruit to God. Though not told, it was as if Abel was the child who operated in the likeness of God. A trait he must have learned from his father. As one reads this story, it is almost impossible not to think of how one child can be so opposite from the other; both being born of the same blood.

The bottom line is that Anger is not an acceptable spirit. It is an uncontrolled emotion that usually causes an undesirable reaction. I know... for those who read the Word says Jesus even got angry. But the key to His anger is that He did not sin. He commands us to do the same.

It was through Pharaoh's anger that he destroyed his own army.

It was through Cain's anger and jealousy that he killed his brother.

It was because of anger that Joseph's brothers wanted to kill him, but sold him into slavery instead.

It was through anger that Judas sold Jesus out.

Countless times throughout the Bible, anger (while acceptable to many) causes the death to others.

The Israelites

The children of Israel were finally released from Egyptian rule. Generations of slavery has crippled the people. After a period (I know not the time) the people began to lose hope and consider their condition normal. The fight for freedom was lost and dreams were destroyed. Thus it was for the children of Israel enslaved to the Egyptians. Four hundred years of incarceration and abuse entangled the people with hate and restlessness. Families were abused, wives taken away, and children separated from parents. This was a true act of terroristic tactics.

Chapter Five - Relationships Challenged

God heard the cry of His people and used Moses and Aaron to free His people from the tyranny of Pharaoh. Hundreds of thousands left the city which left Egypt incapable of building and progressing toward any future. The skilled craftsman and farmers were gone. The curse of this contaminated spirit was finally broken.

It did not take long for freedom to attack the dreams of success. The people started to question leadership; something they had not done before. Their spirits became rebellious because they could not see what they had not seen. God through Moses had led them to the Red Sea with the master plan in mind to show them that He was the Great I Am. The people murmured against Moses and could think of nothing but death, but God had a plan.

You may know the story, if not I invite you to read it in the Scriptures taken from the book of Genesis. Once the people were saved from the hand of the mighty enemy, one who they thought could never be defeated it would stand to reason that God was indeed sovereign. There was rejoicing and singing and people revered the God of their salvation, but it was short-lived.

Mount Sinai proved that once a people's spirit is contaminated it takes the hand of the Almighty God to cleanse that spirit and secure their minds. Moses, their leader, went up into the mountains for a short while to speak with God. Please keep in mind that the people had been in bondage for four hundred years, so thirty days or so should have been a snap for them to hold out. They turned to what they knew to do in the past; a spirit that resonates with us until this very day. Let's have a party; a "knock down drag out" party! Let's be unruly, uncontrolled, unrestrained, have sexual orgies and use spirits to make us limitless in our behavior. Thus the people worshipped gods as they were accustomed to doing in Egypt; they even convinced Aaron to make them a golden calf to worship. These acts of lawlessness rank at the top of the list, yet there was an uncontaminated remnant of Israelites that dared to cross the line.

Joshua was one of those servants. His belief and love for God remained intact along with many others. It sounds all too familiar, and perhaps the pendulum is swinging back toward darkness for some. But praise be to God for those who were overcomers then, and those who yet believe in the Almighty God we serve, today.

Joseph and His Brothers

Hatred and Jealousy are spirits that can consume a person's well-being. This is the case found in the story of Joseph and his brothers. The scriptures reveal to us that God is ready to use willing vessels, especially those who selflessly yield themselves to the work of the Lord. Noteworthy is that the Lord does not always use the eldest of the family to carry out Kingdom work or to gain the inheritance of his father. This fact was apparent with Joseph and also David who was made king of Israel.

In the case of Joseph, his brothers' spirits were contaminated with a combination of jealousy and hatred. God could have chosen any of the brothers, but their innermost being was not able to receive the Word of the Lord. Willing vessels are open to the vision of God and to the work assigned without backlash.

Chapter Five - Relationships Challenged

Joseph clearly understood that he was not the next in line to receive the blessing from his father, yet his heavenly Father used him to save the nation. In so doing Joseph had to go forth against the grain of his brothers and father. He stayed the course enduring the hurt and pain of the cruel treatment of those he loved the most... his family.

Contaminated spirits lash out at common sense and rebuke logic to the point of even threatening to take the life of another. Such is the case with Joseph. Read the Book of Genesis; it will bless your spirit.

Ananias and Sapphira

This is a case of a husband and wife conspiring to deceive Peter as it pertains to their income. Money is known as a source to move people away from humbling themselves to the sovereign deity. The ingredient of greed did not fit the recipe of honesty. Unfortunately Ananias and Sapphira fell in love with the money they were able to acquire. Their spirits fell into the trap of going to extremes to protect the assets they owned. Such a spirit moved them to the point of lying to the authorities about their income. That spirit is still relevant today. For example, people routinely lie about their federal and state income tax returns in order to acquire additional returns or to mitigate taxes owed to the government.

This story is found in the book of Acts the fifth Chapter. We beam in on the caption where Peter is talking to Ananias concerning the selling of his possessions and the amount of money he received from the sale. It is evident as one reads the scriptures that others had gone before Peter to confess, but now it is Ananias' moment to be upfront and honest. He fails the test and turns from the truth to deceive Peter. Little did he know it was really the Holy Spirit that he was dealing with and that his very life was at stake.

Peter must have had pre-instructions from the Lord as to how to deal with those who chose to lie about their business transactions. I make this assumption because Peter did not possess the power to declare death on his own without the power of the Holy Ghost working in him and being in agreement with his actions. Ananias fell in love with his money and decided to chance lying instead of being open and honest. This contaminated spirit would cost him his life. Another thought to add to the story is that Peter already knew the sum of money collected and yet he waited for Ananias to man up. His failure to do so caused him to initiate his own death sentence. I also learned that hearing produces faith and death. The scripture reveals to us that Ananias fell down and gave up the ghost after hearing the words of Peter.

The action of the wife of Ananias (Sapphira) speaks volumes. One can attest from her actions that if you hang around a person that schemes and practices dishonesty long enough that same spirit may just attach itself to you. Though Sapphira did not speak to her husband before having to face Peter, she already must have conspired with her husband to lie to Peter concerning the amount received from selling the property. As with her husband, she too signed her own death sentence by lying to the Holy Spirit. She was afforded the opportunity like many of us to confess the truth and be set free, but instead she refused and was buried beside her husband the same day.

Their deaths were caused by their contaminated hearts saturated by the works of the devil.

Abraham and Lot

The story of Lot and Abraham can be found in the book of Genesis. Abraham is the uncle of Lot and desires nothing more than to satisfy the relationship of the family. Lot has a spirit of greed and ungratefulness. He wants the best of it all and yields to nothing less. The uncle and nephew are faced with a healthy problem and blessed to have an abundance of livestock, so much that their territory had to be increased. Abraham is secure in the Lord and gives little thought to what the future may bring. Lot, on the other hand, walks by sight and not by faith, therefore needs confirmation to lock on his dreams. Lot chooses what appeared to be the finest land. He settles in the cities of Sodom and Gomorrah; a place where all that have an ear to hear of it shake their heads in bewilderment because of the inhabitants' culture.

After their separation the Lord spoke to Abraham and let him know that all the land actually belonged to him. Abraham and his seed would later be blessed because of this faithfulness to God.

Saul and David

As a child David had his first encounter with King Saul. The King's great army's spirit was contaminated with fear as the challenge day-by-day ensued. David, however, had experienced the power of God and walked with a fearless faith. He was perplexed to see that a Philistine was defying the Almighty God. Without hesitation he pleaded to his King to face the enemy, but the King at first denied him the opportunity to war against the giant. David's love for God must have moved King Saul to allow him to face the giant as we should our own giants with confidence. David knew that the bear and lion that he had previously defeated did not come from his own strength but it had to be God that gave him the victory in both cases, so why not now?

He showed his bravery by defeating Goliath, the giant of a man that had frightened the military soldiers Saul commanded. David gathered only five stones and used a slingshot to bring down a giant problem for the Israelite army. This victory would lead to the Kingship of a young man known for his act of triumph.

Chapter Six

THE FAMILY

The family unit has always been threatened in the face of society. Since the first family, referring to Adam and Eve, disruption has been the plan of the enemy. The subtle move of the enemy did not cause Adam and Eve to divorce. However, it did cause them to get divorced from the plan of God. Adam had been instructed through conversation from God to eat of every tree of the garden with the exception of the tree of good and evil or he would surely die. Further details of the scripture reveal that Adam had this discussion with his helpmeet Eve.

The enemy (the serpent) was in tune with the conversation and the test of obedience was on the line. If you know the whole story then you realize that they failed miserably. Not only did Eve eat of the fruit, but she convinced her husband Adam to eat as well. I suspect this is where we earned the term …"misery loves company." We still find ourselves struggling with specific instructions of God and holding true to His covenant. Perhaps it is the curse of Adam and Eve or simply our lack of renewed faith in God. St. Francis used this quote that is common to most.

"Lord, grant me the strength to accept the things I cannot **change**, the courage to change the things I can, and the wisdom to know the difference."

This short prayer to God offered by St. Francis has generated volumes of conversation. The problem as I see it is that we accept too many things that God does not. We allow these things to become part of our daily activities ignoring the Voice of God and the consequences thereof. Our courage and wisdom does indeed come from God, therefore when consulting God we should discern the things He expects of us according to His plan.

In short, we live with many things that are contrary to the Word and plan of God. As children of God we do not have to accept them nor support them.

After being expelled from the garden Adam's and Eve's lives shifted to struggles and difficult times. Being cursed was foreign to them and they did not realize the cunning work of the enemy. Eve had to go through the travail of child-bearing and Adam had to work by the sweat of his brow. Throughout the years man has faced turbulent times simply because of the disobedience in the garden. Families have been destroyed, wars have been fought, and weapons of mass destruction have surfaced. The family unit is fragmented by divorce, blended families, sex slaves of love ones, incestuous relationships, not to exclude those who simply disown one another.

The family unit is beginning to breakdown even more as it moves further and further away from the plan of God. The curse of anger and jealousy has haunted the family for centuries. Nevertheless an enormous number of families have been able to overcome that spiritual separation. It took years but Esau and Jacob were able to mend their differences about the birthright.

Chapter Six - The Family

The Church is a family of believers and like the family unit it has its problems. Reconciling our differences is the key to church growth as it is to family growth. Far too many occasions surface that reveal church family members being at odds with one another concerning mediocre things. Though the vision of the majority of churches is to advance the Kingdom of God, all too often that same vision is crippled by those who *think* they know how to do it better than the anointed one who receives his/her assignment directly from God.

What is the answer and where should the family unit seek peace? Of course the answer is turning back to God and being obedient to His Word. It is much easier said than done. The question is why? Perhaps there is a common substance in all humans that cause us to act outside of the will of God. The substance, simply, known as the "flesh." It is not so much our genetic makeup, but the spirit that we allow to invade our body, mind, and soul.

Most people think of themselves as being good and they might be. They rationalize or affirm that behavior by stating that they do not bother anybody… thinking "I keep to myself, I drink a little bit, I gamble a little bit, I tell a few lies, I cheat occasionally, and curse only when I am angry. When I smoke herb, it is only in my home, other substances I use is for my personal use. What is wrong with that?"

This inward struggle is common to most and has become the acceptable norm. However with this track record of professed sin, heaven will certainly be missed. This is a familiar tune that thousands can sing in harmony. It was prevalent in the days of

Noah and too obvious in the days of Lot. The apostle Paul had this battle evident in his writings;

> *"I do not understand what I do. For what I want to do I do not do, but what I hate I do. And if I do what I do not want to do, I agree that the law is good. As it is, it is no longer I myself who do it, but it is sin living in me. For I know that good itself does not dwell in me, that is, in my sinful nature. For I have the desire to do what is good, but I cannot carry it out. For I do not do the good I want to do, but the evil I do not want to do—this I keep on doing. Now if I do what I do not want to do, it is no longer I who do it, but it is sin living in me that does it."* (Romans 7:15-20)

This is a concern accepting the things that we cannot change. Unfortunately we forget to remember that God can and will transform a man who has a contrite heart. Contaminants do not have to be contained as permanent.

Chapter Seven

LIVING WATER VERSUS WATER TO LIVE

On average, the human body is made up of 70 percent water. The brain is made up of 75 percent water. The blood contains 90 percent water. Therefore we note that water is necessary for the human body to survive. The brain would reflect disorientation without it. The blood would decrease flowing and clotting would result. Without water the human body would dehydrate and eventually go into shock causing weakness and ultimately death.

Today we are facing the challenge of losing one of our greatest commodities…. water. It is simply hard to believe that four decades ago we were drinking water from small running streams of water called creeks (in some places) without the threat of bodily harm. Even tap water in many portions of these United States is not recommended for consumption. It simply is no longer safe; at least that is what we are being told. Water filters and other items to purify water are being sold in epic proportions. Deer Park, Fuji and other brands have taken the corner market on selling water. It is difficult to believe that water covers seventy-one percent of our continent and ninety-five percent of the water source comes from the ocean, yet we struggle to consume it at no cost.

Acceptable Contamination

In the city of Flint, Michigan, the residents are suffering from the lack of clean drinking water and are also exposed to water so contaminated that it creates burns on the skin. Reports reveal that the contaminated source is coming from the lead in the pipes. Further investigation alleges that the governmental authorities knew that the water was contaminated but did not act upon ensuring it was safe for the residents of the city. Unfortunately, accepting marginal levels may and perhaps should cost those who are in the leadership arena to lose their jobs, just as it has caused many of the residents to lose their ability to enjoy the simple ingredient all too common to most...clean acceptable drinking and bathing water.

It is certain that other contaminants are present in our water supply such as microorganisms, which are present in the vast majority of the things we consume, but what is the acceptable safe level? That knowledge is unknown to the common layman and causes many to suffer and pay for the commodity that very well may be safe to drink...water. Don't get me wrong I, too, buy and drink bottled water especially when the area is notably not clean or warnings are posted. The problem is that we as a nation do not raise the flag against those who continually choose to contaminate the water source. It becomes acceptable to dump waste and chemicals into the water system and lessen the cost of doing business. On the other hand, some companies gain by purifying the contaminated water source and selling it back to the public. What a vicious circle.

It has taken decades for America to see that large and small companies disposing of waste material dumped into our water source has caused cancer in some cases and birth deformity in

Chapter Seven - Living Water versus Water to Live

others. We are now paying the price for something we allowed many, many, years ago. Unfortunately the contamination of our water source is a fast moving train perhaps increasing daily and the process is quite difficult to slow down or even stop. Therefore we must suffer the consequences of what we allow to be acceptable.

Chemical and fuel contamination is not the only source of material to degrade our water source. It is known that military vessels, commercial Cruise liners and luxury ships contaminate the oceans by dumping trash and other contaminants into the ocean waters. Several years ago medical supplies were discovered washing up on the shore of the beaches in California. Hypodermic needles and other supplies were among the trash discovered.

Oil rigs are spilling hundreds of thousands of oil into the ocean and how do we clean it up? Of course there are other beach sources with other contaminating chemicals. What do we do? And how do we stop this mass cultural attitude that will soon destroy us all? The answer lies with those who control our resources. The majority of our basic needs are driven by the economical game.

In our society, if money is to be made everyone tries to get onboard. There was a period in which water was being sold and marketed as being purified and it was nothing but water from the tap. So one must wonder if the water is as contaminated as we are being told or not?

Well the verdict is out. We are indeed destroying ourselves and our water supply at a rapid pace. Just recently the entire city of Flint, Michigan experienced a severe water contamination issue initially reported as lead in the water. There is an acceptable amount of lead allowed, however the levels have far exceeded the acceptable table and is now causing chaos throughout the city. If the investigation were revealed to the general public I would suspect that the contamination of the water supply is decades old. The lead in the pipes did not begin only years ago… it took decades to come to this condition. There was a level accepted by those experts that decided on an acceptable lead contamination level. Perhaps as the level increased so did their ban of acceptance. It is the same tactic of the enemy in the garden. The serpent convinced Eve to engage in contaminating her spirit. 'What could it hurt? Just take a small bite. Surely, it will not harm you?'

Now people are rationed cases of drinking water daily and soon the supply of distribution will run out. Once the water source is no longer able to be purified the people will have no other choice but to abandon their homes and livelihood and seek other places to dwell. Unfortunately, this is not the cure to the water problem as through the river the contamination will travel to invade the next township.

The root of the problem stems from the hand of man and the destruction will also come from that same hand.

What can we do to stop this senseless wave of self - destruction and contamination of our resources? Too many will disagree but the answer is still in being obedient to God and applying His principles.

The Living Water… Christ, our Lord, will soon come to settle the score of man verses God. While at the well with the woman a conversation ensued. The woman came to get water

Chapter Seven - Living Water versus Water to Live

for her physical well-being and Jesus offered her Living Water. It was quite a shift from what she was accustomed to hearing from any man. Jesus certainly knew His purpose and the woman's purpose for gathering water. She thirsts for what no man could give. She sought a substance that could satisfy her bodily needs; the mineral that could wash away the body odors, but could not cleanse the soul. That longed for ingredient was living water.

Jesus used the term living water in the scriptures to describe the adrenaline rush of knowing who He really is. Secondly, He expresses that the essential substance common to all mankind will never have to be sought after again if you are connected to Him.

> *"But whosoever drinketh of the water that I shall give him shall never thirst; but the water that I shall give him shall be in him a well of water springing up into everlasting life."* (John 4:14)

> *"He that believeth on me, as the scripture hath said, out of his belly shall flow rivers of living water."* (John 7:38)

Jesus is the decontamination agent that will cleanse the bodies of all who will accept Him as the Savior of the world. The purification process begins with acceptance of His Deity and confession follows.

> *"That if thou shalt confess with thy mouth the Lord Jesus, and shalt believe in thine heart that God hath raised him from*

Acceptable Contamination

the dead, thou shalt be saved. For with the heart man believeth unto righteousness; and with the mouth confession is made unto salvation." (Romans 10:9-10)

It is a struggle for man to believe that Jesus is the solution to our issues; therefore He is ignored and set aside. We toil and work our fingers to the bone with little results and celebrating temporary repairs. Albert Einstein said it best when he said:

"Problems cannot be solved by the same level of thinking that created them."

It is past time to seek the Lord!

Chapter Eight

DRIFT

(Doing Right If Forced To)

Drift occurs in a person's life when an outside interruption enters into a set plan and causes that person to deviate from the initial mindset. Somehow their original plan is abandoned and adjusted to fit into the box of "doing right if forced to" do so.

We are moved by what we see, feel, taste, hear and experience. Many times the sense of sight leads us down the wrong path. So many times we ignore the things that should raise an alert flag and focus on those things that really should be ignored. In these United States, perhaps we call it that simply because the states bump each other in places, or perhaps it is because we are connected through idealism. In any case it does not take long to find out just how united a country really is. During the election season, we are free to vote but showered with differences on how the country is to be run and by whom. We have witnessed that it does not take much to divide us. Murder cases, specifically the O. J. case divided a nation and still the wounds are healing.

Even in the year of 2015 our great nation struggled with the ghost of the past. We as a nation continue to accept the things that separate us from the love of God and man. Recently the state symbol of the State of South Carolina voted to take down the rebel flag after 54 years of representing painful memories of inhumane acts toward fellow man. It was appalling to see far too many Americans holding on to a wicked past and demonstrating their concern not for history, but for what rested in their hearts on that sad day of July 10, 2015.

It was a celebration of sorts, but the victory does not lie in the Confederate Flag's removal. The minds of the people have to be changed and that will undoubtedly take decades to swing if not another century. The sweltering expressions of hatred appeared to drip from the faces of those who simply didn't want to let go of a symbol that represented notorious injustice to mankind.

I focused on the comments made when reporters interviewed people randomly. One man who appeared to be a baby boomer, professed "they have their own church and we have ours, they ought to be happy now. Immediately my mind registered who the "they" are. Another commented "we ought to be allowed to hold on to a symbol, though it represented racism and hatred, because our forefathers fought in that war. These testimonials confirmed that the state has been contaminated with ignorance and locked in on the ghost of the past which is all too acceptable.

Far too many people in this concentrated area simply refused to forget the past and renew their minds with the words given by our Lord that we are all precious in His sight.

For nearly five and one half decades the people of South Carolina ignored doing the right thing. As a former resident, it was well known that your chances of competing for equality were narrow and that it was just the way it was. This inbred behavior was stamped by the "Rebel flag" flown over the

Chapter Eight - Drift

Capitol of the state and unfortunately, though fought by the people for years, the statement remained. We are of the mindset of being superior. The harsh words still ring out "remember your place."

The shedding of blood gave credence to the awful act of erecting the flag and sadly it took the shedding of blood to lower it – the cruel act of murdering nine people worshipping the Lord. A single young man committed the act, but it was really perpetuated by those who supported wickedness and hatred. It simply took too long for a nation that is rich in resources and possesses some of the most brilliant minds in the world to wake up and smell the coffee. I cannot imagine the pain endured by those who worked in the state capitol all those years having to pass by the constant reminder that you are less than someone else.

Even those who were not of the Black race had to feel the presence of the evil acts and reminders of the old South. Far too often we habituate to things that should not be and fall into commonness of accepting what we choose not to change. I have coined the term DRIFT (doing right if forced to) to remind those who have an ear to hear that we do not have to remain in a contaminated state if we take action.

I love the song phrase "when you have done all you can do to stand…STAND." It is like a medicine injected directly into the veins of my very being. It assures me that though the world tries to contaminate your spirit …. RESIST. Do not give in to the things of the world and make your election sure. Anchor yourself and secure the mind that:

Acceptable Contamination

"I can do all things through Christ that strengthens me."
(Philippians 4:13)

Here we are fifty plus years later "forced" to take down a symbol that divides a nation to this day. This flag was erected to protest the Civil Rights movement. Some of the supporters were crying and stating that they would defend the flag until they died. How shallow is the mind when one continues to live in the past and defend it because their forefathers fought in the battle. What happened to righteousness and justice? Should we sanction ropes and hold a ceremonial feast with them for those who were hung by them? I pray not!

Racism

Racism is one of the society strongholds. It is a subtle way of the enemy to separate the Church and divide the common faith that man should have in God. The unrest and blatant works of evil against another race is all too easy to figure that the enemy has his hand in the process.

Racism creates an atmosphere in some people that depicts them as a powder keg ready to go 'Boom!' Race discrimination acts as the catapult for anger and violent actions years down the road. As with several of the national racial attacks (both black and white) the problem of man's inhumanity toward man has lasting effects. Lives are cut short. Dreams are destroyed. Families are broken and hope is fractured if not completely shattered.

Chapter Eight - Drift

This infectious disease has interwoven itself into law enforcement and many others who are sworn to protect and serve the people. Things are spiraling out of control as we witness daily the executions of law officers and civilians on the street. Fortunately with the help of social media, there are very few criminal acts that go unnoticed by everyday citizens or strategically placed cameras. It is all too surreal to awaken and listen to the news, local, national and international concerning a terrorist act or blatant murder. It is close to the disturbing rule of 'an eye for and eye.'

The killing has become so common that it is almost expected and unfortunately accepted as the norm. The weapons of mass destruction are now viewed as an internal problem and not one of the war enemies. We are trapped with the gun law of the land. On one hand it is a necessary evil to possess a weapon to protect oneself against the escalating acts of criminal mischief. On the contrary, weapons are exploited to serve as the devil's workshop: "to rob, kill and destroy lives. A balance must be reached, but the political minds to be are at odds in settling what should be considered a common sense matter. Tougher weapon possession laws are a must!

It does not take long to find these weapons in the hands of those who disregard human life and center their eye through the scope targeting others that do not fit into their racist mindset. It is a form of terrorism.

As a young man racism was a way of life. It seemed the world was not made for people of color, but then it could not be right as you studied the Word of God and learned that Jesus loved all. Where and why did this hatred exist? What source or manner of man perpetuated its continuance?

Much too young to understand the cruelty in the world I was exposed to "whites only" and other discriminatory acts that were accepted as normal. Separate restaurants, movie theater sections, school buses and so many other demeaning contaminated spirits roamed the land.

You could actually visualize the anger that rested in the faces and minds of men and women. The American dream was far too unreachable for African Americans. The future did not hold any promises and the past was too troubling to recall. Once a person is seated in this frame of mind, hope becomes dim and logic is distorted. It is as though the individual justifies his or her unacceptable behavior because the future (in their opinion) is so bleak.

Far too many people experience this phenomenon. Far too many accept it as a normal way of life.

Far too many refuse to help their fellow man to see a better way. Far too many simply give up too soon. Far too many are exposed to what the real world is not. Far too many cut their lives short with drugs and other mind-altering substances ignoring the possibility of a successful life.

People on the other side of the vicious act of racism are exempt from feeling the throbbing painful effects of its deep cutting fury. The nonvisual blows felt by the individual are at times too much to handle and it causes defense mechanisms to expose themselves. Those who do not learn coping skills are sadly incarcerated, scarred for life, or killed for making the wrong choice.

Chapter Eight - Drift

Same-sex Marriage

Same-sex marriage is yet another disease to divide the Church. It seems to be a political issue that spills over into the Church. The battle is turned from the sin and beamed in on state and church debates.

The latest decision of the highest court in the land to uphold same-sex marriages in all fifty states in the USA rocked the foundation of America. In doing so, the very fabric of those who hold marriage in highest esteem between one man and one woman was ripped into shreds.

The atmosphere set by same-sex couples creates confusion among the land and like many other sins divides instead of uniting. Children are confused because they now have two fathers or two mothers that declare to them that they were born that way. It must be underscored here that this action undermines the scripture that declares:

> *"Therefore shall a man leave his father and his mother, and shall cleave unto his wife: and they shall be one flesh."* (Genesis 2:24)

> *"Now for the matters you wrote about: It is good for a man not to marry. But since there is so much immorality, each man should have his own wife, and each woman her own husband. The husband should fulfill his marital duty to his wife, and likewise the wife to her husband. The wife's body does not belong*

to her alone but also to her husband. In the same way, the husband's body does not belong to him alone but also to his wife." (1 Corinthians 7:1-4)

"Wives, submit to your husbands as to the Lord. For the husband is the head of the wife as Christ is the head of the church, his body, of which he is the Savior. Now as the church submits to Christ, so also wives should submit to their husbands in everything. Husbands, love your wives, just as Christ loved the church and gave himself up for her to make her holy, cleansing her by the washing with water through the word, and to present her to himself as a radiant church, without stain or wrinkle or any other blemish, but holy and blameless. In this same way, husbands ought to love their wives as their own bodies. He who loves his wife loves himself. After all, no one ever hated his own body, but he feeds and cares for it, just as Christ does the church – for we are members of his body. "For this reason a man will leave his father and mother and be united to his wife, and the two will become one flesh." This is a profound mystery--but I am talking about Christ and the church. However, each one of you also must love his wife as he loves himself, and the wife must respect her husband." (Ephesians 5:22-33)

These scriptures and others are clear and simply DO NOT support same sex relationships. To ignore the commandments of God is voluntary rebellion.

The results of such relationships continue to confuse children who are subjected to such misguided conduct.

Chapter Eight - Drift

The Church continues to be under the microscope and is highly scrutinized as it works toward reconciliation in many areas. The separation and cultural division is affecting society and the message to those who do not know nor understand the spiritual experience. We work together and shop together and vacation and play together, but our worship experience continues to be divided.

We must remember and acknowledge the Scripture which identifies and clearly provides us with the mode of operandum of the enemy.

John 10:10 KJV
*"The thief cometh not, but for to **steal**, and to kill, and to **destroy:** I am come that they might have life, and that they might have it more abundantly."*

Legalized Prostitution

Legalized Prostitution is now being looked upon as a necessary evil. Though it is one of the oldest occupations/professions in the world, it does not make it right to legalize it just because it continues to be a problem in society. Robbing banks has also been a long-term problem in society for those who want to take shortcuts in getting rich, but we do not make it a legal action simply because we cannot stop the criminal minds that continue to commit the act.

Selling one's body does in fact "kill" the spirit of true relationship and intimacy with the intended purpose created by God. When a person accepts lowering their standards to a point of offering their body for money it fits the motive of the adversarial plan. Once again there is a move affront to legalize what God has clearly declared to be an abomination.

Marijuana

Marijuana is yet another substance that is spiraling out of control and sought to be legalized in many states as well as internationally. The claim is that it has ingredients that act as a medical relief. It is known to alter behavior and cause hallucinations which result in harm to the individual. Those who have experimented with the use of it are now regretting the experience which by their own testimony led to other drug use. Other testimonies of those who used the substance say it caused them to do things that ended up scarring their lives forever. Common from the mouths that tried marijuana is my family was "destroyed," my job was lost, and my life is now in ruins as a result of my addiction to using the drug. It did in fact "kill" my drive to work and pursue my dreams. Any drug that has the capability to "steal" your joy must be avoided. However once again the populist believes that if you cannot control it legalize it.

Living Together

One of the most popular trends facing us today and in times past is "living together." It is all too common and some have even embraced the act as being common law and acceptable to society. Perhaps it is, but not to the Lord. When speaking to those who find themselves in this common relationship most

Chapter Eight - Drift

reply that everyone is doing it and there is no harm done. In some cases the live-in relationships are occurring in the homes of the parents. It is almost too hard to think or imagine what goes on behind closed doors.

One should not have to be forced to do the right thing. If we do not continue to ignore the wrongs of the world…If we do not accept the things we really can change…If we bow down and seek the Face of God, things can and will change.

Let us not simply DRIFT away and fold to the ways of the world.

Chapter Nine

A FAD WITH NO FAVOR

Couple Swapping

Ashley Madison, a recently developed society breakout is the media site that encourages married couples to seek outside affairs. Unbelievably this site is reported to be flooded with millions of participants. Many of them are those who the public would not expect to be on the list of players. Yes. You guessed it already – Christian leaders and the exposure of such participation caused them to resign their position as leaders in the Church. There are just too many people that continue to fall into the evil trap of the enemy. His mode of operandum remains the same, but is often painted as something new.

"The thief cometh not, but for to steal, and to kill, and to destroy: I am come that they might have life, and that they might have it more abundantly." (John 10:10)

Even in this day and time when evil is raging criminal minds troll the internet exploring opportunities to take advantage of wild ideas such as this. Though there is nothing new under the sun, creative foolishness continues to intrigue thousands that may otherwise walk away from the idea of wrong-doing. That is not to blame technology for the wicked hearts of men and women, it is however an added source to reach out into extreme parts of the world to seek good and evil actions.

Tragically, it is known that it is only a matter of time when couples enter this type of interaction that someone's life will be shattered either by disease or even the ultimate, death. This dating service is a modern form of legalized prostitution and many will fall prey to its grasp. It is yet another vice to "destroy" the family unit and create havoc with the order in which the Lord considers sacred...

How do we avoid the contaminants from infiltrating the intended design of God's plan? The simple answer is to stick with the plan of God and refrain from compromising just to draw people into the Body of Christ. Simple compromising the Word of God leads to unbelievable mindsets. Let's examine a few:

Jesus during His ministry on earth did not have to turn over tables in the temple and upset the apple cart sort to speak of those who were selling goods; at least they were in the temple. He did not have to contest the Scribes and Pharisees for their vile teaching; at least they were religious. He could have remained neutral throughout many instances of the scriptures and kept silent on issues, thereby avoiding persecution and crucifixion. However, that was not the plan of God then, neither is it now. Saints must carry the torch of righteousness.

I recall once studying the process of how gold is refined. This precious metal is known to represent the Divine. In its raw stage it contains contaminants much like us. It has to go through a process to separate the good metal from the unacceptable attachments around it. The craftsman knows as he

Chapter Nine - A FAD with No Favor

begins the process that it will take a little time to purify the metal. Gold contaminants depreciate its value. So is it with the Word of God. The diluted Word of God weakens its power and turn good men and women away from the truth of Holy living.

Extracting Gold

The process of removing gold from the rocks is simply amazing. I am surely no expert in retrieving the gold nor do I claim to know even the slightest bit about the process, but after reading extensively here is what I discovered. There are several processes to extract gold. This is one that I found interesting.

Water is a special ingredient to assist in mining or acquiring gold. Imagine that! The Living Water of Christ does the same work. The gold is separated by the worker using small carbon grains added to a processing tank. The gold then attaches to the carbon and continues through a process called electrowinning or electroextraction. As I understand the process this action allows gold to be drawn out from other metals. To reach the refining process flux is added and smelting is introduced.

So how do you know what gold is worth? Gold is measured by the karat age which refers to how much gold exists versus other alloy substances. I have learned the higher the karat, the more expensive the gold. Twenty-four percent (karat) parts in gold is considered 100 percent gold. Other gold metals are measured by this formula.

When speaking of karatage in the past I only equated it to jewelry. Perhaps this scale will educate you as well.

The Worth of Gold

24 karats = 100 percent gold
22 karats = 91.75 percent gold
21 karats = 87.5 percent gold
18 karats = 75 percent gold
14 karats = 58.5 percent gold
12 karats = 50.25 percent gold
10 karats = 42 percent gold
9 karats = 37.8 percent gold
8 karats = 33.75 percent gold

> *"And I will bring the third part through the fire, and will refine them as silver is refined, and will try them as gold is tried: they shall call on my name, and I will hear them: I will say, It is my people: and they shall say, The LORD is my God."* (Zechariah 13:9)

As one can see, things associated with the Divine require a process that cannot be overlooked or provided shortcuts to meet the goal. Today the vetting process is a must for those who proclaim to be the sons and daughters of the Living God. Though the process may be rigorous, once it is completed and the believer stands the test of resistance, I believe God is pleased.

Perhaps it is prudent to look at this using the natural eye. Let's refer back to the process of gold.

Chapter Nine - A FAD with No Favor

We, like the gold in its raw stage, or in human terms "our unsaved stage" are shaped in inequity. That is, we are surrounded and intertwined with the impurities of life. In order to see the real beauty of who we are there must be a refining process (a new birth).

Here is the difference: our refinement is determined by our own desire process. We choose to be 24 karat gold in the sight of the Lord or something less than. That's right! We are still considered gold even if we are eight karats. But why rest at the bottom of the barrel when in Philippians 4:19 we know that He can and will supply every one of our needs according to His riches in glory?

Romans 12:1-2 says it best:

"I beseech you therefore brethren, by the mercies of God, that ye present your bodies a living sacrifice, holy, acceptable unto God, which is your reasonable service. And be not conformed to this world; but be ye transformed by the renewing of your mind, that ye may prove what is that good and acceptable, and perfect will of God."

It just sounds like being refined and seeking the purities of God to reach the twenty-four karat level.

We are set for a course of destruction if we continue to accept the contaminated spirits that lurk the atmosphere. A great awakening is necessary to turn the hearts of men back to God. Be refined, redeemed and renewed! Allow God to extract the things that are not of Him. It may take vigorous action but stay on the potter's wheel, endure the turn and become a new

Acceptable Contamination

creature. He can and will decontaminate your spirit. He did it for me and will certainly do the same for you.

www.ingramcontent.com/pod-product-compliance
Lightning Source LLC
Chambersburg PA
CBHW070547300426
44113CB00011B/1818